Automated Security Analysis of Android and iOS Applications with Mobile Security Framework

Automated Security Analysis of Android and iOS Applications with Mobile Security Framework

Ajin Abraham

Contributing Editor
Henry Dalziel

AMSTERDAM • BOSTON • HEIDELBERG • LONDON
NEW YORK • OXFORD • PARIS • SAN DIEGO
SAN FRANCISCO • SINGAPORE • SYDNEY • TOKYO

Syngress is an imprint of Elsevier

SYNGRESS.

Syngress is an imprint of Elsevier
225 Wyman Street, Waltham, MA 02451, USA

Notices
Knowledge and best practice in this field are constantly changing. As new research and experience broaden our understanding, changes in research methods, professional practices, or medical treatment may become necessary.

Practitioners and researchers must always rely on their own experience and knowledge in evaluating and using any information, methods, compounds, or experiments described herein. In using such information or methods they should be mindful of their own safety and the safety of others, including parties for whom they have a professional responsibility.

To the fullest extent of the law, neither the Publisher nor the authors, contributors, or editors, assume any liability for any injury and/or damage to persons or property as a matter of products liability, negligence or otherwise, or from any use or operation of any methods, products, instructions, or ideas contained in the material herein.

ISBN: 978-0-12-804718-7

British Library Cataloguing-in-Publication Data
A catalogue record for this book is available from the British Library

Library of Congress Cataloging-in-Publication Data
A catalog record for this book is available from the Library of Congress

For Information on all Syngress publications
visit our website at http://store.elsevier.com/Syngress

ELSEVIER   Book Aid International   Working together to grow libraries in developing countries

www.elsevier.com • www.bookaid.org

CONTENTS

ABOUT THE AUTHORS

Ajin Abraham is a Security Engineer with 6 + years of experience in Application Security including 3 years of Security Research. He is passionate on developing new and unique security tools than depending on preexisting tools that never work. Some of his contributions to Hacker's arsenal include OWASP Xenotix XSS Exploit Framework, Mobile Security Framework (MobSF), MalBoxie, Firefox Add-on Exploit Suite, NodeJsScan etc to name a few. He is the cofounder of X0RC0NF, an annual security conference conducted in Kerala. He has been invited to speak at multiple security conferences including ClubHack, NULLCON, OWASP AppSec AsiaPac, BlackHat Europe, Hackmiami, Confidence, BlackHat US, BlackHat Asia, ToorCon, Ground Zero Summit, Hack In the Box and c0c0n.

Henry Dalziel is a serial education entrepreneur, founder of Concise Ac Ltd, online cybersecurity blogger and e-book author. He writes for the Concise-Courses.com blog and has developed numerous cybersecurity continuing education courses and books. Concise Ac Ltd develops and distributes continuing education content [books and courses] for cybersecurity professionals seeking skill enhancement and career advancement. The company was recently accepted onto the UK Trade & Investment's (UKTI) Global Entrepreneur Programme (GEP).

INTRODUCTION

Let's talk about automated Security Analysis of Android & iOS Applications with Mobile Security Framework.

CHAPTER 1

The Mobile Application Pentest

Mobile Application Pentest

- Needs a dedicated environment.

- Devices or Configured VM.

- Tools to access and extract data.

- Tools to perform security assessment.

- Manual Code Review

- Assessment should cover OWASP mobile & Web Top 10.

- This same process follows when a new release/update for the mobile application happens.

Consider a typical mobile application pentest. You need to set up a dedicated environment. You should either have devices or configured virtual machines, like Android or iOS virtual machines or emulators. Then you need the right tools to access and extract the data in transit like HTTP(S) proxies, SQLite viewer for viewing SQLite DB files, and all those things etc. Again you need another set of tools for performing security assessment of mobile applications and another important aspect of mobile application pentest is a Manual Code Review. So you have to do the Manual Code Review; if it is an Android binary you have to decompile it, extract the source code, then do a code review on the source code. Or if it's a white box testing where you have access to the source code, you have to go to the source code and perform a security code review. Again the assessment should cover OWASP mobile top 10 and the OWASP Web Top 10 in case of hybrid application. So these days, mobile applications are mostly hybrid, they have both the mobile component as well as the web component in them. So the vulnerabilities that affect the mobile phase as well as the vulnerabilities that affect the web space are applicable in this context.

Again the same process follows when a new release or update for the mobile application happens. This is really a cumbersome process. Whenever there is an update or a new major version release or change, you have to go through the whole process. And again it's not really an easy job. You have to have the entire environment ready and set up so that you can start testing a new application or a version update. So this really is a hectic process to setup and maintain the testing environment. And in this space comes the importance of mobile security framework.

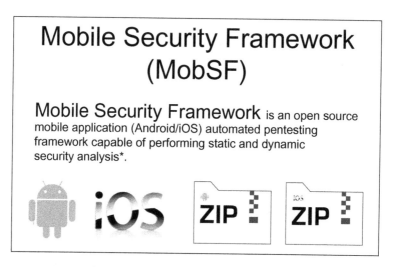

So Mobile Security Framework is an open source mobile application—Android/iOS automated pentesting framework capable of performing static and dynamic security analysis. The current version supports Android, compressed source code zip file, iOS compressed source code zip file; so any can be the input. As of now the framework only supports dynamic analysis of Android binaries. You can download it from github: https://github.com/ajinabraham/Mobile-Security-Framework-MobSF/, which is the project page of mobile security framework. The framework is multiplatform compatible; so as of now it runs in Windows, Linux, and Mac. When it comes to Linux, the tested and supported Linux operating system is Ubuntu.

When it comes to security assessment, there are a lot of security tools or products out there that works from the cloud.

Hosted in your environment. Your application and data is never sent to the cloud.

There is no cloud
It's just someone else's computer

So there is the image that you don't have to worry about things like setting the environment and configuring the things manually. Applications deployed in cloud will do everything from their end and will give you a neat clean report. But for most of the organizations, due to policy or compliance reasons they don't really want to upload their data, code, and application to cloud.

For them, cloud is nothing, it's just somebody else's computer. So there comes an advantage of mobile security framework. Everything is hosted in your environment. Well in that case, you only have to set up mobile security framework in your environment once. Once it is set up, you don't have to worry about anything. So from the next time onwards just give it the APK, IPA, or the source code so that it will do the security analysis and give your report. You don't have to go through all the process of setting up your environment, configuring it, finding the correct tools, capturing the data, and then again doing the security analysis. The framework automates everything for you.

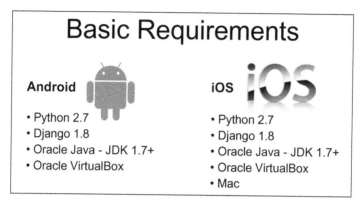

So the basic requirements to run mobile security framework (MobSF) are, if you want to do security analysis of Android application that means if you want to do security analysis of Android binaries, or source code, you need: Python 2.7, Django 1.8, Oracle Java − JDK 1.7 or higher and you need Oracle VirtualBox as well. In case of iOS application, you will need: a MacBook or a Mac device to set up mobile security framework so that it can support security analysis of iOS applications as well. Again it also requires Python 2.7, Django 1.8, Oracle Java − JDK 1.7+, Oracle VirtualBox, and as I said before, a Mac.

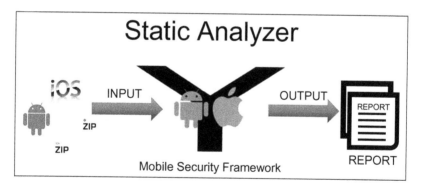

So here I have a picture of how static analysis functions in mobile security framework. You can provide Android binaries, iOS binaries and compressed Android or iOS source code as the input to MobSF. The mobile security framework will perform a static analysis and then give you the output. MobSF also allows you to generate a pdf report from the output. This report will contain the list of vulnerabilities identified by mobile security framework.

CHAPTER 2

Configuring Mobile Security Framework for Static Analysis

Configure MobSF for Static Analysis

- Download the latest release : https://github.com/ajinabraham/Mobile-Security-Framework-MobSF/releases

- Extract it to
  - Windows: C:\MobSF
  - Linux (Ubuntu) : /home/<username>/MobSF
  - Mac: /Users/<username>/MobSF

- Install Python

- Linux and Mac users make sure Oracle Java is installed and make it your default java.

- pip install –r requirments.txt

- python manage.py runserver

So here is a quick recommendation: in case of windows, extract the zipped package to C:\MobSF. In case of Linux, you can extract it into /home/ < username > /MobSF. In case of Mac, you can extract it into /Users/ < username > /MobSF. The reason being, if you try to extract it into some other different path, it may happen that some whitespaces might get introduced to the path name or when mobile security framework runs, it may detect a very long path that can cause problem with the applications or tools run by MobSF. So it's better to extract it into the directories as mentioned above.

Again you have to install Python; that is, Python 2.7. Also you have to install Oracle Java – JDK 1.7 or higher. In case of Linux and Mac, users might have some java installed by default and most probably that's not Oracle Java. To run MobSF and its dependencies, you need to install Oracle Java 1.7 or higher. So you have to download

Oracle JDK from Oracle website according to the platform that you are using, then install it and make it the default Java. And once that is done, you have to satisfy the dependencies of Mobile Security Framework. For that you can navigate to the base directory of mobile security framework in command prompt/terminal and then issue the command pip install−r requirements.txt which will download and install all the python dependencies that mobile security framework requires. Note that if the pip command fails while installing the dependencies, you must install all the python packages mentioned in **requirements.txt** separately to ensure the proper working of MobSF. This is a very important step. And once that is done, you are ready to go. You can go inside the mobile security framework's root directory and then issue the command python manage.py runserver. This will start your server at http://127.0.0.1:8000. Now you have successfully configured static analyzer in MobSF. You can also refer to the documentation available on the github project page. Here you can go to mobile security framework, project page, go to wiki, and then select documentation from the right tab and that will show you the complete documentation. So you can follow the detailed documentation. Now let's download mobile security framework and configure the static analyzer. Let's open the zip file and let's extract it to C:\MobSF. Go to your C-drive, create a new folder; name it MobSF, the case does not really matter here; select the directory and then extract. And take the command prompt and go to C:\MobSF from here you can see the requirement.txt so these are the different dependencies that needs to be satisfied. Let's issue the command pip install−r **requirement.txt**. In case of Windows your pip is located in C:**Python27\Scripts**. Let's go to that directory and issue the command. Well I already have all the dependencies installed, it didn't take much time but if it is a fresh installation; for you it will take some time to download all these dependencies and install them. So once that is done you are ready to go. You can issue the command python manage.py **runserver** and this will start the server in 127.0.0.1:8000. If you want to start the server in some other port number, you can give a space to the previous command and mention the port number. So let's start the server in default port and it will automatically find the JDK location in Windows. And once everything is done you can see that MobSF has started the server at 127.0.0.1:8000. Let's go to that URL. So now we can see the web user interface of Mobile Security Framework; this is how you download and configure mobile security framework.

CHAPTER 3

Static Analysis

Static Analysis
Android Binary
• INFORMATION GATHERING
• DECOMPILE TO JAVA & SMALI
• PERMISSION ANALYSIS
• MANIFEST ANALYSIS
• JAVA CODE ANALYSIS
• ANDROID API INFO
• FILE ANALYSIS
• URLS, EMAIL, FILES, STRINGS, ANDROID COMPONENTS
• REPORT GENERATION

Let's have a deep look into static analysis. In the case of Android binary, mobile security framework will perform the following things. It performs the information gathering on file size, the file hashes and all those information. It will decompile the binary into Java and Smali source code. It will do a permission analysis from a security perspective; it will also do a security analysis on the manifest file, and it will also do a code review or code analysis on the decompiled Java code; and it will also give you information about the Android APIs used by the application. It performs a file analysis and it will extract the URLs, emails, files, strings, and Android components, and finally you can generate a neat report.

In case of Android source code, we don't want to decompile it into Java or Smali because we already have the source code. The rest of the things are pretty much the same. Let's go back to mobile security framework. Click on upload and analyze then select an APK. Now the APK is being uploaded, depending on the size of the APK and the time varies. You can check for the progress in command prompt. So you can see the detailed process over here.

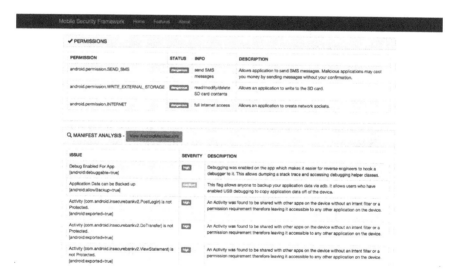

Once everything is done you will get a Static Analysis result page where you can see the file information, the application information; the nature of the code, distribution and access to the source code, the Java as well as the Smali source code, and the downloads. Then you can download a PDF report as well. It also has an option to start dynamic analysis. That will be covered later; so if you click on download PDF report, it will actually generate a PDF report and present it before you. So once the PDF rendering is completed you can access the report. It also shows you the certificate information, the permissions that are being used by the application and a detailed table that shows the different permission, their description and the status. Also it performs a static security analysis on AndroidManifest.xml. It also performs code review and points out the possible security issues and the severity as well as the files that contain the insecure code. You can click on any of the files to see the contents.

Now if you scroll down, you can see the Android APIs that are being used by the application. So you'll get a good idea about what the application is supposed to do. On the bottom you can see the static URLs that are found in the binary, and it will also show you the emails extracted from the binary. So the emails are also listed and the corresponding files are shown here. It will also do a file analysis and show you the report. If there is any string found, it will also list all the strings here. And at the bottom you can see the different files in the binary archive and the different Android components like activities, services, receivers, content providers, and libraries.

STATIC ANALYSIS OF ANDROID SOURCE CODE

Now let's see how we can scan an Android Source code. Here we have the source code of Android InsecureBank, a deliberately vulnerable Android application to teach Android security. The application is written in Android Studio. We can identify that from the application directory structure. As of now mobile security framework supports two major IDEs, which are used to develop Android applications. One is Eclipse and the other one is Android Studio. So this particular Android InsecureBank application is built using the Android Studio IDE. So in order to perform the static analysis on the source code, select all the files in the root directory then compress it into a zip file. So now you get app.zip. Take your browser and navigate to MobSF's main page. Click on upload and analyze and select app.zip, which is the compressed source code of InsecureBank Android application. It will perform security analysis and give you the results, which are similar to that of Android binary, the only difference is that here there is no need for decompilation into JAVA or SMALI code because we already have source code access. Also the results are actually stored in the database. So once a successful scan is done, the results are stored in the database and from the next time onwards, if you actually try to do the security analysis of the same application, MobSF will fetch the data from the database and present it before you. In case if you want to do a completely fresh new scan, you can select rescan option at any point of time. Once the scan is completed again the results are pushed into the database.

Static Analysis

- iOS - Binary
  - BASIC INFORMATION
  - BINARY ANALYSIS
  - FILE ANALYSIS
  - LIBRARIES
  - **REPORT GENERATION**
- iOS - Source
  - BASIC INFORMATION
  - CODE ANALYSIS
  - iOS API INFORMATION
  - FILE ANALYSIS
  - URL, EMAIL, FILES, LIBRARIES
  - **REPORT GENERATION**

So for performing static analysis of iOS application, you need to install and configure mobile security framework in a MacBook. For iOS binary apps, we can obtain basic binary information. Again we can perform binary analysis to uncover security vulnerabilities. MobSF also performs file analysis and shows you the different libraries used by the application; and finally a PDF report is generated. For iOS source you will again get basic information, a static security code analysis; the iOS API information; file analysis; URL and email extraction; information about the files and the libraries used in application and again a PDF report. Let's see that in action.

So here I am running mobile security framework; you can just go to the browser and select "Upload and Analyze" and select any IPA, IPA is an iOS binary; so once I upload that you can see that analyzing has started.

Static Analysis

Once the analysis is complete you will get a page, which shows the information about the application. So it lists out the various information about the binary, the application and performs a security binary analysis, which points out the different security vulnerabilities. And then it also performs a file analysis where it shows the plist and other files. And they even list the different libraries, which are used by the application and the files in the binary package.

STATIC ANALYSIS OF iOS SOURCE CODE

Now let's see how we can perform a static analysis of iOS source code. So here, I have the source code of an iOS application; this is an XCode project. As of now mobile security framework supports applications made with XCode. Let's select all the files in the root directory and then compress it and form a zip archive. Archive is created, let's go to mobile security framework and upload the zip file. So once the analysis is done, you will get a report that looks similar to the static analysis report of an iOS binary. In addition to that you can see code analysis being performed and also it will give you an idea about the different iOS APIs that are used by the application. The URLs and emails that are hardcoded in the source code will be listed. And following that you can see the file analysis where it points out the plist files, certificate, or key files hardcoded inside the application etc. and information about libraries if any of the libraries are present and finally the list of files inside the zip archive.

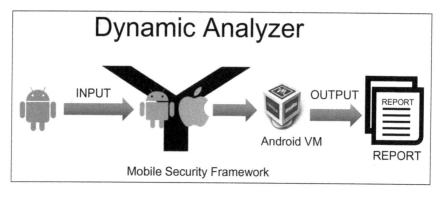

The current version of mobile security framework only supports dynamic analysis of Android binaries. The input to mobile security framework's dynamic analyzer is an APK, and mobile security framework will spawn an Android VM which is configured with its own agents to capture all the information, data, and perform security analysis in the background and then the user or the security analyst can navigate through the different flows of the application. Wherein in the background the agents collect all the necessary information from a security point of view. And once everything is done, the analysis output is sent to mobile security framework and a report is generated.

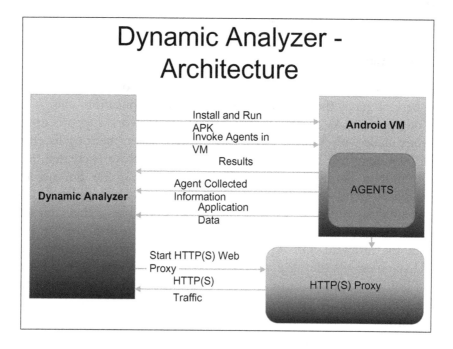

Let's have a look into the high level architecture of dynamic analyzer. Dynamic analyzer initially will spawn an Android VM, which is preconfigured with our agents and tools. It automatically installs the application, that is, the Android binary, and runs it. And it will invoke the agents, which already exist inside the VM. Well now it's up to the user or the security tester to navigate through the different flows of the particular Android application. The dynamic analyzer will also start an HTTPS web proxy parallel to all this in order to capture the web traffic. So once the VM environment is ready, the user or the security tester can navigate through the different flows of the application. The agents will capture the data in the background and perform security analysis on the data that is collected, and once the analysis is done, as a final step the application data created by the application inside the VM will be sent over to the dynamic analyzer so that it can perform further security analysis on the application data. Once everything is done you will get a report.

Dynamic Analysis

- SCREENSHOT
- CAPTURE HTTP(S) TRAFFIC
- ACTIVITY TESTER
- LOGCAT and DUMPSYS
- DYNAMIC API MONITOR
- DYNAMIC URLS and EMAILS MONITOR
- APPLICATION DATA DUMPER
- FILE ANALYSIS ON APPLICATION DATA
- REPORT GENERATION

So these are the major features of dynamic analysis. You can take screenshots, capture the web traffic, we also have a module called exported activity tester to find out exposed activities and then it will dump the LOGCAT and DUMPSYS logs; and there is a dynamic API monitor like the one which actually determines what are the API calls made by the application at run time. Also there is a dynamic URL and email monitor which will capture all those URLs and emails which were dynamically created. And we have the application data dumper that will dump the application data, created by the application inside the device. Moving on, there is a file analysis module that performs file analysis on the application data fetched from the device, and finally a report can be generated.

CHAPTER 4

Configuring MobSF for Dynamic Analysis

In order to configure the dynamic analyzer, you have to follow the MobSF wiki. Visit https://github.com/ajinabraham/Mobile-Security-Framework-MobSF/wiki/Documentation to access the wiki. Let's see how to do that. Go to the mobile security framework Github page. Here you can open the wiki link. So scrolling down you can see Configuring Dynamic Analyzer; so dynamic analyzer actually needs a host system, which is having at least 4GB of ram and with full virtualization support. If either of the two is not available things might not work properly.

To Configure Dynamic Analyzer we need 4 things.

- VM UUID
- Snapshot UUID
- Host/Proxy IP
- VM/Device IP

You have to download the latest MobSF VM OVA file from the link available in the Wiki and you should be having Oracle VirtualBox installed. Now you can open VirtualBox and go to **File -> Import Appliance** and then select the downloaded VM OVA file.

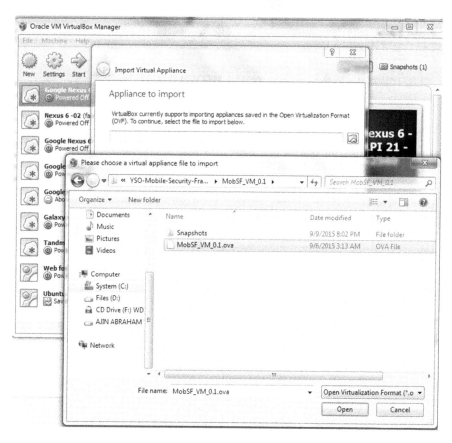

So here is OVA file, select it, continue, import. So this will import OVA file into your system. Once the OVA import is completed, you will find MobSF VM listed in VirtualBox.

Right Click on MobSF VM and choose Settings. Now we have to configure the network settings properly. The VM needs two adapters. **Adapter 1** should be enabled and attached to **Host only Adapter** and you should remember the name of the adapter. We need that to identify the Host or Proxy IP.

Adapter 2 should be enabled and attached to the **NAT.**

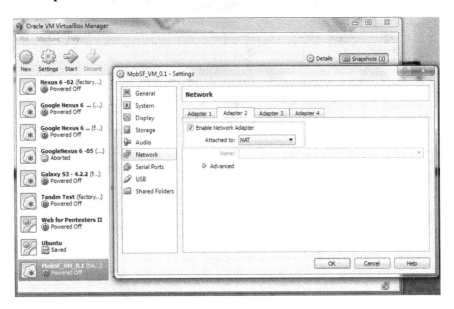

Once you have configured the network, do a double check. Go to Network tab and make sure that **Adapter 1** is enabled and is **Host only adapter,** just note down the name of the adapter. In this case it will be

VirtualBox Host Only Ethernet Adapter #5. We need this name to identify the Proxy IP or Host IP. Switch to **Adapter 2** tab and make sure that it's enabled and attached to **NAT**. So this looks good. Click on ok and once your network properly is configured, you can start MobSF VM. Let's power on this VM. While the VM is booting up, you can see an IP. And that is the IP of the VM.

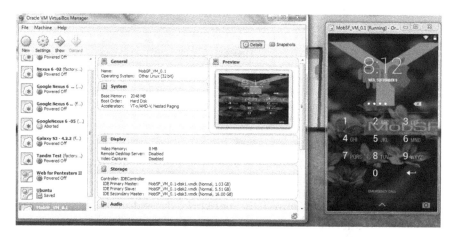

You can see that 192.168.**106**.101 is the IP address allotted to this VM and this is referred as the VM IP/ Device IP.

Once the VM boots up, it will present a lock screen. The password for the lock screen is 1234.

Now you can obtain the Host IP or the Proxy IP. In Windows, take your command prompt and issue the command **ipconfig.**

```
Ethernet adapter VirtualBox Host-Only Network #5:

   Connection-specific DNS Suffix  . :
   Link-local IPv6 Address . . . . . : fe80::ad53:d578:d01c:acle%46
   IPv4 Address. . . . . . . . . . . : 192.168.106.1
   Subnet Mask . . . . . . . . . . . : 255.255.255.0
   Default Gateway . . . . . . . . . :
```

You can see that *VirtualBox Host-Only Network #5* is the Host only adapter for the VM is having an IP **192.168.106.1**. This is your Host IP/Proxy IP and **192.168.106.101** is your VM/Device IP.

In case of MAC/Linux, open a new terminal and issue the command **ifconfig** and look for the adapter name.

```
vboxnet0: flags=8843<UP,BROADCAST,RUNNING,SIMPLEX,MULTICAST> mtu 1500
        ether 0a:00:27:00:00:00
        inet 192.168.56.1 netmask 0xffffff00 broadcast 192.168.56.255
```

You can see that *vboxnet0* (in MAC) is the Host only adapter for the VM and the corresponding IP is 192.168.56.1.

Now let's get back to the booted VM. Go to your WiFi settings and set the Proxy IP/Host IP in the Proxy Hostname field and put the port number as 1337 or anything of your choice which is not really used by any other application in the Host OS.

Let's go to Settings and double tap the WiFi option, press and hold the WiredSSID and that will show you a window where you should click on Modify network. Now under proxy, choose manual option then move down and set the Proxy/Host IP in the Proxy hostname field. That is 192.168.**106**.1 and the port number as 1337. Save it and then once that is done you have to navigate to the home screen of the MobSF VM. Let's click on the home screen wait for 30 seconds and then create a snapshot of the VM.

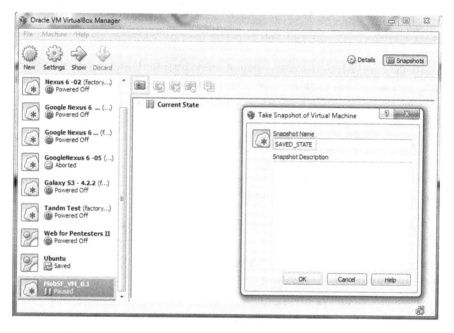

So select the VM, then go to Snapshots tab and then click on the take a new snapshot button and give a name to it. Wait until the snapshot is created. Once the snapshot is created, close the MobSF VM.

Now get back to VirtualBox window and right click on MobSF VM and select **Show** in **Finder** in case of Mac or **Show** in **Explorer** in case of Windows.

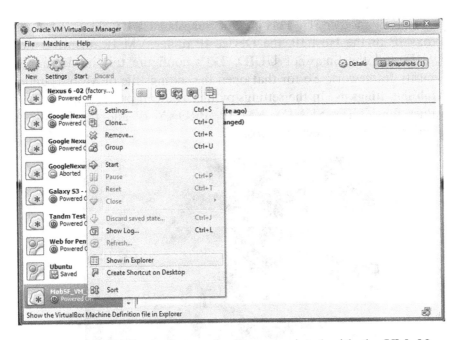

This will actually show you the files associated with the VM. Now inside the directory there is a vbox file, open it using any text editor to obtain your VM UUID and Snapshot UUID. So there is a **MobSF_VMX.X**.vbox file, open it with any of your favorite text editor.

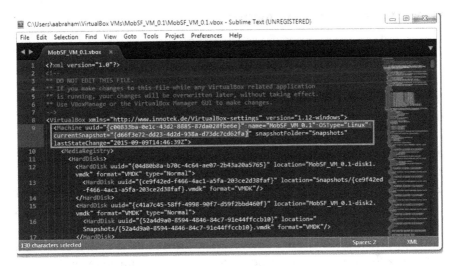

So under the VirtualBox attribute, there is a **Machine** UUID. This is your **VM UUID**; and after that there is a **currentSnapshot** and it points to another ID. This is your **Snapshot UUID.** So we have the Proxy IP or the Host IP, the Device IP or the VM IP, then the VM UUID and the Snapshot UUID. Let's configure this inside mobile security framework. So for that open the settings file of MobSF under **MobSF/settings.py**. In the settings.py file, you can provide appropriate values for UUID, SUUID, VM_IP, PROXY_IP and the PORT as obtained from the previous steps.

```
#VM SETTINGS
#VBoxManage showhdinfo "MobSF_VM_0.1-disk3.vdi"

#VM UUID
UUID='621937f5-90c4-49c3-9a08-249dcdd53f3b'
#Snapshot UUID
SUUID='d919f470-10e6-4dc5-8012-9aff30dd704d'
#VM/Device IP
VM_IP='192.168.106.101'

#PROXY SETTINGS
PROXY_IP='192.168.106.1' #Host/Server/Proxy IP
PORT='1337' #Proxy Port
```

Now all the 4 parameters that we need for performing dynamic analysis are available. Save the settings.py file and run your mobile security framework to perform dynamic analysis.

DYNAMIC ANALYSIS OF ANDROID APPLICATION

While mobile security framework is running, go to your browser; let's go to the mobile security framework tab, click on upload and analyze; select an APK, upload it and wait for the static analysis to complete. You can check the status of the process in the console. Once it is done the report is generated. This is the static analysis report. Now click on start dynamic analysis button, which will spawn the snapshot of MobSF VM and once the VM successfully starts up you can actually click on create environment to create a testing environment. You can check the progress of the process in console. You can see that HTTPS proxy is running and the APK is being installed and it's opened. Now let's go to the dynamic analyzer page. You can click on start exported activity tester to check for the exported activities or you have other options like start activity tester. You can take screenshots as well and all the information is actually available in the console. You can even execute ADB commands. If there is an error, that will be displayed over here. Once everything is done you can click on finish and mobile security framework will do a security analysis on the data collected by the agents as well as the application data dump and will give you the final report.

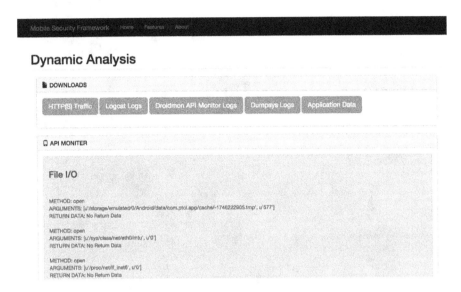

API Monitor

Activity Tester

HTTPS(S) Traffic

```
 1
 2
 3    REQUEST: POST https://ssl.google-analytics.com/batch
 4    Content-Length: 230
 5    Accept-Encoding: gzip
 6    Content-Encoding: gzip
 7    Connection: close
 8    User-Agent: GoogleAnalytics/4.0.6 (Linux; U; Android 4.4.2; en-us; Samsung Galaxy S4 - 4.4.2 - API 19 - 1080x1920 Build/KOT49H)
 9    Host: ssl.google-analytics.com
10    Content-Type: application/x-www-form-urlencoded
11
12
13    ;O8-U&u:xb/J<~*e@81L>9Am][7V    -!Q=s%C;IXt8E\aN8umTGt#
14    d:r*JP.dÇ:B,_e1Xg8
15    Tf;!c]%yf|
16    R5o⊠}oN't9
17
18
19    RESPONSE: 200 OK
20    Alternate-Protocol: 443:quic,p=0
21    Content-Length: 35
22    X-Content-Type-Options: nosniff
23    Expires: Fri, 01 Jan 1990 00:00:00 GMT
24    Server: Golfe2
25    Last-Modified: Sun, 17 May 1998 03:00:00 GMT
26    Connection: close
27    Pragma: no-cache
28    Cache-Control: no-cache, no-store, must-revalidate
29    Date: Wed, 09 Dec 2015 06:51:24 GMT
30    Alt-Svc: clear
31    Content-Type: image/gif
32
```

Decrypted HTTPS Traffic

SQLite Database

data/data/vlokal.vdelivery/app_webview/Cookies

data/data/vlokal.vdelivery/app_webview/Web Data

XML Files

Other Files

data/data/vlokal.vdelivery/app_webview/Cookies-journal

data/data/vlokal.vdelivery/app_webview/Web Data-journal

data/data/vlokal.vdelivery/app_webview/Cache/18bf977abd4b94d5_0

data/data/vlokal.vdelivery/app_webview/Cache/18bf977abd4b94d5_1

data/data/vlokal.vdelivery/app_webview/Cache/18bf977abd4b94d5_2

Application Data Dump from the VM

So this is how the dynamic analysis result will look like. You can download the HTTP traffic, the logcat logs, Droidmon API monitor logs, the Dumpsys logs, application data etc. And the API monitor shows the APIs that are being called by the application at run time, the networking calls being made, the binder calls being made, File IO operation, and so on.

If you have previously chosen for exported activity tester, then the result will be shown here. Same with the activity tester and the screenshots will also be listed below that. And then it will also capture the URLs and emails that are dynamically generated. Then the complete HTTPs traffic will also be shown with all the request and response bodies. And after that the application data will be dumped from the VM to the dynamic analyzer, which includes all the SQLite databases, shared preference XML files and other files. SQLite database files are later parsed and presented as readable text files. You can click on the file and that will show you the contents of the DB. Then you have the XML files, which are probably the shared preference, and the rest of the files are categorized under other files. So this is how the dynamic analysis is done with mobile security framework.

CHAPTER 5

Case Studies

Let's do some real world case studies.

All the APKs used for Case Study are available here: https://goo.gl/9yAJho.

ANDROID PREMIUM SMS MALWARE ANALYSIS

The first one is an Android Malware Analysis. So we will be analyzing a malware, which actually sends SMS to premium SMS number using mobile security framework's dynamic analyzer. Let's do that; let's upload the APK. So here we have SMS.apk. And there is not much information on the code analysis. This maybe because the binary is obfuscated. Okay, let's do dynamic analysis. And create an environment for testing. So the application opens and it is asking to send SMS to some number. So since it is a newer version of Android, it's presented with a choice whether to allow this application to send the SMS or not. If it is a previous version of Android, it won't even show this prompt. So the SMS will be sent to a number, which is basically the malware behavior and it's a malware that sends SMS to premium numbers. Let's click on finish. Now if you scroll down you can see that SMS method, sendTextMessage was invoked and you can also see the arguments passed into the method. So this verifies that the application try to send SMS to premium SMS numbers at run time. So this is one of a typical example of doing malware analysis with mobile security framework.

APPLOCK MITM PASSWORD RESET VULNERABILITY

Now let's see another case study: AppLock MITM Password Reset Vulnerability. This vulnerability was identified by mobile security framework. Okay, let's see what's the vulnerability. So this is static analysis report of AppLock. AppLock is an Android application that allows you to put a lock screen over other Android applications. Let's do the dynamic analysis. Create an environment and now you can actually navigate through the different flows of the application. So AppLock is open; you can set the password and then provide an email to which the password reset token needs to be sent. You can save the email, so once that is done AppLock is ready to go. So if you want to navigate to the flows of the application, like you can lock SMS, then let's try accessing the SMS. There it asks for the password. So the only option you have there, other than that, is to click on the forget password, where it actually shows the Forgot password view with an option, send the code to security email. So you click on that and the reset code has been sent to your email. All right these are the different flows of the application. Now let's finish the dynamic analysis. If you scroll down to the traffic section, you can see interesting things like all the traffic made with the AppLock server is actually in HTTP and there is no HTTPS being used. You can see all the API calls and their response. If you scroll down, you can see an interesting API call made to "http://applock.domobile.com/servlet/applock." This is a password reset call where it actually sends email as a parameter to the call and later investigations reveal that what happens in the background is that the applock.domobile.com server will send a token to the email address specified earlier. Irrespective of the registered email—you can give any email here and the MD5 of this token will come as the response to this call. So how this reset mechanism work like, whenever someone gives an email the server will actually create a random reset token, send it to the specified email and take the MD5 hash of that particular token and send it back to the response of the API call so that the application can verify that reset code by calculating it's MD5 hash. So the problem with this system is that it is actually using HTTP which means MITM attacks are possible and the second thing is that there is no validation or verification of the email parameter at the server side so if an MITM happens, the hacker can give his email ID here to obtain the reset token and later, and reset the password for the particular user.

Let's see how much we can exploit this. I have a Genymotion emulator and I am just installing the AppLock application. Now I have to set a password for AppLock; just confirming the password again. And now we have to set the security email; the email to which the reset code should be sent; save it and AppLock is installed. Let's lock gallery. Now let's go to gallery and it's actually protected by

AppLock. Let's click on "Forgot Password" and you can see the email ajin25@gmail.com there, which is not editable. Let's open up an MITM proxy to exploit this particular scenario I have modified the proxy. If you scroll down you can see the code

If *self.*request.url== "***http://***applock.***domobile.com/servlet/applock***"

That is the URL to which AppLock sent the password-reset request and what happens is that when that URL is invoked, the MITM proxy will replace the email with xenotix.in@gmail.com which is some email address that the attacker controls. This is the xenotix.in@gmail.com mail inbox; it's empty. Now in order to stimulate the MITM attack, I have to provide proxy address in the WiFi settings. So let's go to WiFi settings and modify the settings. Now here we have to give the proxy address. Let's take a new terminal and issue the command **ifconfig** and my IP address is 192.168.0.7. Okay let's give the proxy IP, give any port number, and save it. Now let's run our proxy; proxy is running. Let's take the gallery app; click on forgot password and then click on send the code to security email. Now you can see that the MITM proxy has done something in the background and the app is actually showing the message that it has successfully sent the reset token. The proxy actually replaces the email with attacker controlled email, xeno-tix.in@gmail.com. If you go and check xenotix.in@gmail.com inbox, you can see a mail from AppLock server that contains the password reset code. You can enter the password reset code; and click on reset password and now you can set a new password. This is how you can reset AppLock's password by performing MITM attack.

BYPASSING PIN IN WHISPER ANDROID APPLICATION

Let's do another case study. Bypassing PIN in Whisper Android Application. Let's take mobile security framework and perform a static analysis on whisper APK. Let's wait for the analysis to complete, ok now we have the static analysis report. Let's investigate on this. So if you move down you can see that there is couple of results under mani-fest analysis with severity high mentioning like sh.whisper. WWhisperBrowserActivity, sh.whisper.WDiscoverActivity etc. are not protected because the Android exported attribute is set to true that means other applications can involve this activity. Moving down we can find some interesting activity like WInbox activity and

WNotification activity. So these activities correspond to—the first one corresponds to the inbox and the second one corresponds to a notification activity. In fact whisper is having an option to protect this notification and inbox activities using a PIN. But since these activities are exported, an attacker can actually invoke these activities from other malicious applications and bypass the pin feature. So mobile security framework has uncovered this vulnerability that allows an attacker to access protected activities. Let's see how we can exploit this.

This is a proof of concept for PIN bypass in whisper, so here I have the whisper application and if you go and check the settings you can see that a 4-digit pin is set. So now if you click on the messages it will ask you to enter the PIN. But if you go to notification, it again will ask you to enter your PIN. For example, click on notification, it's asking for the PIN. So basically there is a way to bypass this pin, because these activities corresponding to messages and notifications are exported. So whenever you mark an activity as exported that means other applications can access it. So even if there exist a pin protected view, it doesn't matter, I can actually bypass that. So I'll show you an example. This is a proof of concept, application, click on that; click on PIN bypass and see notification. So it will show you the whisper notifications. These are my whisper notifications and the same way, if I go back and click PIN bypass and read message, it will actually show my whisper messages.

These are some of the real world case studies with mobile security framework.